REGIONS OF THE UNITED STATES

EXPLORE THE MID-ATLANTIC

by Kristine Spanier, MLIS

pogo

Ideas for Parents and Teachers

Pogo Books let children practice reading informational text while introducing them to nonfiction features such as headings, labels, sidebars, maps, and diagrams, as well as a table of contents, glossary, and index.

Carefully leveled text with a strong photo match offers early fluent readers the support they need to succeed.

Before Reading

- "Walk" through the book and point out the various nonfiction features. Ask the student what purpose each feature serves.
- Look at the glossary together. Read and discuss the words.

Read the Book

- Have the child read the book independently.
- Invite him or her to list questions that arise from reading.

After Reading

- Discuss the child's questions. Talk about how he or she might find answers to those questions.
- Prompt the child to think more. Ask: Have you been to different regions in the United States? If so, which ones? How are they similar to or different from one another?

Pogo Books are published by Jump!
5357 Penn Avenue South
Minneapolis, MN 55419
www.jumplibrary.com

Library of Congress Cataloging-in-Publication Data

Names: Spanier, Kristine, author.
Title: Explore the Mid-Atlantic / by Kristine Spanier, MLIS.
Description: Minneapolis, MN: Jump!, Inc., [2023]
Series: Regions of the United States
"Pogo books." | Audience: Ages 7-10
Identifiers: LCCN 2021049031 (print)
LCCN 2021049032 (ebook)
ISBN 9781636907147 (hardcover)
ISBN 9781636907154 (paperback)
ISBN 9781636907161 (ebook)
Subjects: LCSH: Middle Atlantic States–Juvenile literature.
Classification: LCC F106 .S74 2023 (print)
LCC F106 (ebook) | DDC 974–dc23/eng/20211102
LC record available at https://lccn.loc.gov/2021049031
LC ebook record available at https://lccn.loc.gov/2021049032

Editor: Jenna Gleisner
Designer: Molly Ballanger

Photo Credits: Maglara/Shutterstock, cover (top); Andrei Medvedev/Shutterstock, cover (middle); Mihai_Andritoiu/Shutterstock, cover (bottom); Javen/Shutterstock, 1; Svetlana Foote/Shutterstock, 3; Zack Frank/Shutterstock, 4; North Wind Picture Archives/Alamy, 5; dkfielding/iStock, 6–7; Jon Bilous/Shutterstock, 8–9; Christopher Barnard/Alamy, 10; Andrea Izzotti/Alamy, 11; Pete Oxford/Minden Pictures/SuperStock, 12-13tl; Hiroya Minakuchi/SuperStock, 12-13tr; Yann-HUBERT/iStock, 12-13bl; Richard Herrmann/Minden Pictures/SuperStock, 12-13br; Joel Carillet/iStock, 14-15; Damien VERRIER/Shutterstock, 16; Karen Foley/Dreamstime, 17; ironwas/Shutterstock, 18-19; Steve Heap/Shutterstock, 20-21tl; Eliyahu Yosef Parypa/Shutterstock, 20-21tr; dszc/iStock, 20-21bl; Winston Tan/Shutterstock, 20-21br; gangliu10/iStock, 22t; Thomas Kloc/iStock, 22m; Luciano Mortula - LGM/Shutterstock, 22b; Edwin Verin/Shutterstock, 23.

Printed in the United States of America at Corporate Graphics in North Mankato, Minnesota.

Title Page Image: Niagara Falls, New York

TABLE OF CONTENTS

CHAPTER 1

HISTORY AND LOCATION

Where is the birthplace of the United States? English **settlers** chose land on the Atlantic Coast. They called it Jamestown. The year was 1607. This area later became part of Virginia.

Jamestown, Virginia

Indigenous people already lived here. But more settlers came. They started 13 **colonies**. Many Revolutionary War (1775–1783) battles were fought here. Colonists gained **independence** from England. Delaware became the first state.

Delaware is one of seven states in the Mid-Atlantic. The others are Maryland, New Jersey, New York, Pennsylvania, Virginia, and West Virginia. Washington, D.C., is in this **region**, too. It is a **district**. The **federal government** meets here. Members meet at the U.S. Capitol Building.

TAKE A LOOK!

Which states are part of the Mid-Atlantic? Take a look!

Civil War (1861–1865) battles were fought in this region. One in Gettysburg, Pennsylvania, lasted three days. This war helped end **slavery**.

DID YOU KNOW?

Harriet Tubman helped **enslaved** people escape the South. The system was called the Underground Railroad. Some found freedom in northern states. Others went to Canada.

Gettysburg Battlefield

CHAPTER 2

GEOGRAPHY AND WILDLIFE

The Potomac River is in this region. It is called the Nation's River. Why? Mount Vernon was built on its banks. It was President George Washington's home.

Almost every state in the region touches the Atlantic Ocean. West Virginia and Pennsylvania do not. Chesapeake Bay divides Maryland. It is the largest **estuary** in North America.

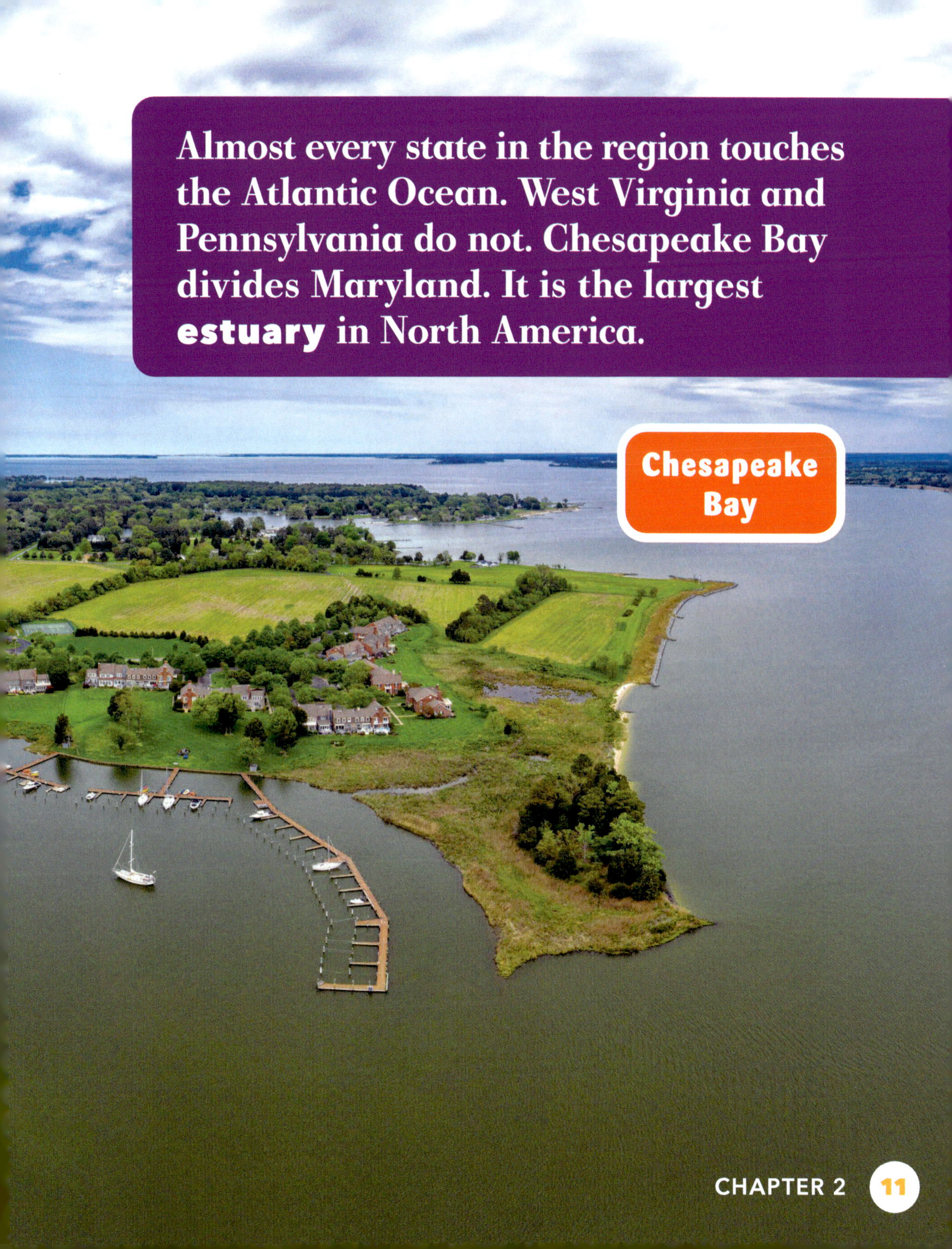

Many ocean animals can be seen along the coast. Sailfish have large fins. Stingrays and sharks swim here, too. You might even spot a blue whale!

sailfish

stingray

blacktip sharks

blue whale

APPALACHIAN TR.-NORTH
GRAYSON HIGHLANDS
STATE PARK

The Appalachian Mountains run through the region. They start in Canada and end in Alabama. A trail is along this mountain range. It can take seven months to hike it all. Some people hike only part of it.

WHAT DO YOU THINK?

Several mountain ranges make up the Appalachians. They include the Catskills, the Blue Ridge Mountains, and the Alleghenies. Are there mountains where you live?

CHAPTER 3

DAILY LIFE

New York City is the most **populated** city in the region. It is also the most populated city in the country. It is filled with skyscrapers.

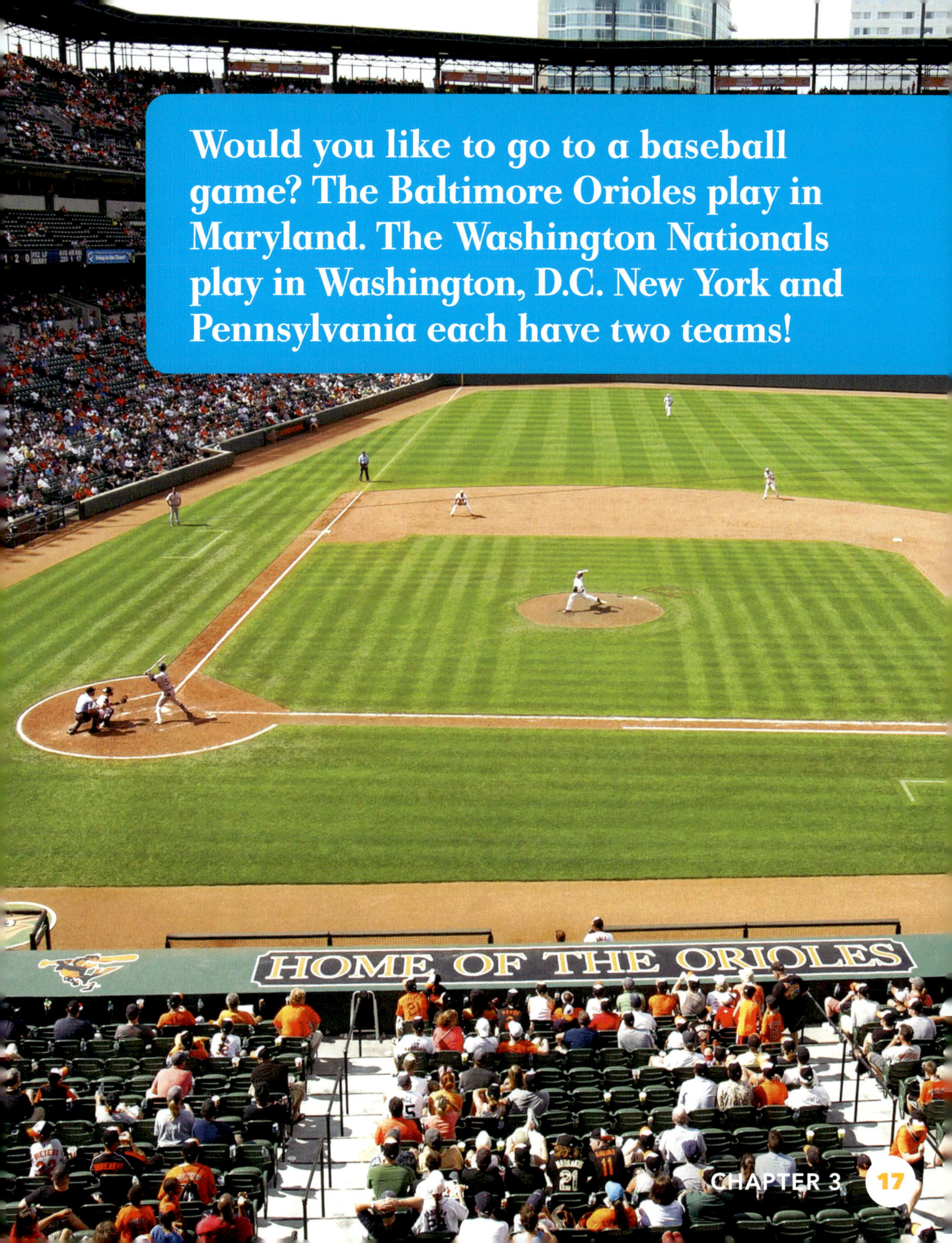

Would you like to go to a baseball game? The Baltimore Orioles play in Maryland. The Washington Nationals play in Washington, D.C. New York and Pennsylvania each have two teams!

Many people in this region **mine** for coal. Others work in banking. **Tourism** is popular. People can also earn a living by fishing.

TAKE A LOOK!

What are some of this region's top **industries**? Take a look!

The region's weather changes with the seasons. Cherry blossoms bloom in spring. People head to the beaches in summer. Leaves turn bright colors in fall. People ice-skate in winter.

There is much to see in the Mid-Atlantic. Would you like to explore it?

WHAT DO YOU THINK?

The Cherry Blossom Festival is in Washington, D.C., every year. What festivals take place where you live?

Washington, D.C.

Ocean City, Maryland

West Virginia

New York City

MID-ATLANTIC REGION

Location: eastern United States

Population (2021 estimate): 60,330,895

Most Populated City in Each State:
Wilmington, DE
Baltimore, MD
Newark, NJ
New York City, NY
Philadelphia, PA
Virginia Beach, VA
Charleston, WV

Top Industries: farming, fishing, manufacturing, mining, tourism

Average High Temperature:
mid-80 degrees Fahrenheit (30 degrees Celsius)

Average Low Temperature:
mid-20 degrees Fahrenheit (–4 degrees Celsius)

Major Mountain Ranges: Adirondack, Allegheny, Appalachian, Blue Ridge, Catskill

Highest Point: Mount Rogers, VA, 5,729 feet (1,746 m)

Major Waterways: Finger Lakes, Lake Erie, Lake Ontario, Allegheny River, Delaware River, Hudson River, James River, Rappahannock River, Susquehanna River, Patapsco River, Potomac River, Chesapeake Bay, Erie Canal

Major Landmarks: Niagara Falls, Statue of Liberty, National Mall, Mount Vernon, Gettysburg Battlefield

PHILADELPHIA, PA

DELAWARE RIVER, NJ

STATUE OF LIBERTY, NY

GLOSSARY

colonies: Areas over which a different country or state has control.

district: An area or region.

enslaved: Owned by another and treated as property.

estuary: The wide part of a river, where it joins the ocean.

federal government: The central power of the United States.

independence: Freedom from a controlling authority.

Indigenous: Of or relating to the earliest known people to live in a place.

industries: Businesses or trades.

mine: To dig up minerals that are in the ground.

populated: Having people living in it.

region: A general area or a specific district or territory.

settlers: People who make a home or live in a new place.

slavery: A system in which people owned other people and treated them as property.

tourism: The business of serving people who are traveling for pleasure.

Liberty Bell, Philadelphia, Pennsylvania

INDEX

TO LEARN MORE

Finding more information is as easy as 1, 2, 3.

1. Go to www.factsurfer.com
2. Enter "exploretheMid-Atlantic" into the search box.
3. Choose your book to see a list of websites.

FACT SURFER